HISTORY
OF
HALF-
BIRDS

A HISTORY OF HALF-BIRDS

poems

CAROLINE HARPER NEW

MILKWEED EDITIONS

Published 2024 by Milkweed Editions
Printed in Canada
Cover design by Mary Austin Speaker
Cover photo/illustration by John James Audubon
Author photo by Steven Kardel
24 25 26 27 28   5 4 3 2 1
First Edition

Library of Congress Cataloging-in-Publication Data

Names: New, Caroline Harper, author.
Title: A history of half-birds : poems / Caroline Harper New.
Description: Minnepolis, Minnesota : Milkweed Editions, 2024. | Summary:
"Selected by Maggie Smith for the 2023 Ballard Spahr Prize for Poetry,
this debut collection of poems explores the aftermath of history's most
powerful forces: devotion, disaster, and us."-- Provided by publisher.
Identifiers: LCCN 2023028084 (print) | LCCN 2023028085 (ebook) | ISBN
9781571315304 (trade paperback) | ISBN 9781571317186 (ebook)
Subjects: LCGFT: Poetry.
Classification: LCC PS3614.E5636 H57 2024 (print) | LCC PS3614.E5636
(ebook) | DDC 811/.6--dc23/eng/20230710
LC record available at https://lccn.loc.gov/2023028084
LC ebook record available at https://lccn.loc.gov/2023028085

Milkweed Editions is committed to ecological stewardship. We strive to align our book
production practices with this principle, and to reduce the impact of our operations in
the environment. We are a member of the Green Press Initiative, a nonprofit coalition of
publishers, manufacturers, and authors working to protect the world's endangered forests
and conserve natural resources. A History of Half-Birds was printed on acid-free 100%
postconsumer-waste paper by Friesens Corporation.

CONTENTS

PART I

WIDDERSHINS

PART II

PARLOR TRICKS

PART III

HYPOTHETICAL MOONS

Dear fossil, I am sorry for the light.

—Traci Brimhall

A HISTORY OF HALF-BIRDS

PART I

WIDDERSHINS

THE ELEPHANT MOTHER

Every year there's a flood in this Georgia delta,

sometimes two or three. I know a woman who rowed to the hospital

to give birth. I know a woman named Carol, who instead opened a home

for elephants. Carol spent years searching for the perfect land, then years more

to find an elephant. She prepared: a series of thick-walled pipes, driven four feet deep

in the clay, enforced with a steel top rail, and waited, until Bo finally

arrived. The circumference of his ankles—five feet plus—

was much bigger than the females she'd prepared for, and so

Carol began all over. Re-fencing her hundred acres of thick swamp

and blue spring and cornfield for her thirty-four-year-old

circus retiree. Now, the biggest concern? He disappears

into the Georgia pines, and not even Carol can find him. Flashlight

prying through the night swamps, nettles seizing at her calves.

Asian elephants have a lifespan of forty-eight years in the wild,

even less in captivity, of which Carol is acutely aware. What counts

as motherhood? For a horse, you must dig a pit

nine feet deep and borrow a tractor to drag it by the ankles; not unlike

pulling a stubborn calf from the womb. You can use the same chains.

In the case of a hurricane, tie your name around your horse's neck

and open the gates. Hope for the best. Carol knows elephants can swim

up to six hours, but had anyone ever taught him?

She never wanted children. She only wanted

to set something free, as she calls *Bo!* circling the fence

in the overgrown dark, checking two, three times each bolt.

WIDDERSHINS

Her hands are in my mouth
when my dentist and I discover our common love of bones.

Our professions, both of them, are at odds with the fact that once formed,
enamel cannot repair itself. She concerns herself with caramel
for the same reason I track the skeletal layout of human fingers
in whale flippers, in possum toes.
How the alligator split from the flamingo
by accident. There is no reason

to think dinosaurs weren't also soft and pink, says the paleontologist. After all,
our fear of birds is ancient: hinged ankles, swivel toes, a wishbone.
There is no reason

to wish ourselves extinct, yet if left to instinct, humans
walk circles counterclockwise. Think of the hippodromes. The middle of the desert.
The word for this in witchcraft

is *widdershins*, meaning counter
to the sun—unlucky, unless intentional, in which case
it's a curse. We used to have a dog

that chased shadows in frantic, endless circles until we had to tie him up.
Still, one day, I pulled from his soft giddy mouth a songbird, wet and whole and

presumably dead. No thumping on the chest or warm sugar water could rouse it.
I set it on the fencepost while I dug a tiny grave,
but when I reached for the body

it was gone. Dancing widdershins
can summon the supernatural, defined as beyond
scientific understanding. The body was merely in shock. There is no reason to doubt

witchcraft, says the paleontologist. *We study the past to know the future,*

                                          and yet, our fear
is as ancient as the possum in the headlights. The familiarity
of the small pink hands. The dentist says I can wait
                          to have this dead tooth pulled from my mouth
                  as long as I can ignore it.

THE ARCHAEOLOGY MAGAZINE

I am cutting every gold
thing I find from this archaeology magazine.

Dead things left by living things
or living things left by dead.

I used to study bones. His

were particularly splendid, soldered
like stained glass, at once Baroque and
Paleolithic. The cortical layer fractured

into maps and spells, a pattern
almost biblical. Warmth

may be an indicator of
something living or killed.

In the magazine is a map
of the igneous faults which mark
the mass extinctions.

That which ended the Cretaceous era
shrouds the desert where his mothers tilled pearl
millet. The Triassic over mine's tobacco. This irony

requires that I call him. He points out

the irrelevance: my mothers were not
in South Carolina 200 million years ago.

I point out that 66 million years ago
his mothers were nocturnal, arboreal,
insect-eating mammals.

Nevertheless, my mothers buried enough
in South Carolina to displace
any teeth capped in gold.

Nevertheless, our mothers must have been
beautiful beings to decimate the earth
to skeletons.

I am cutting every gold thing
from this archaeology magazine

to decoupage into paintings, each a portrait
of his deposition. I stretch

his nervous system on pins into a scripture
that must make him twitch because he calls

in the early morning hours. *I can feel you*
putting a hex on me, a jinx, something.
    Cut it out. I slide his bones

into my pocket, unfold the gold things
more gently, apologize—

    Sorry, my love, I didn't mean to wake you.

He cuts, *You can't call a killed thing*
                            love.

GARDEN OF EVE

When Adam pointed
at the storms, he saved their names
for women, knowing women split
the sky before he even sprouted legs.
Eve first broke the soil, but Alice
was the first one named, the very first
to stake her claim, despite
Adam's intent. He must have
been real nice to Alice, who kept her head
down and hardly hit. Must have
really fucked Barbara, who breezed in
full bitch and blow; set the tone
for what middle sisters could be—
Camille cranked and crazed and
Dolly hot with daddy grudges dealt
on deadbeat Adam, who didn't
even notice Edna slipping in
and out 'round shattered orchards,
smashing peaches to mirror
her older sisters. So say
the aunties. We weren't there.
We don't enter this story
'til Florence—born
with a maternal urge
to eat. She pulled us by our hair
from muddy womb and planted
us back in Eve's overgrown bed
face first, feet pointing sky. She watered us
back into the Gulf and picked us
from her teeth like salted pork.
Swaddled us as tightly as you should
wrap piglets in a house built squalor
and squeal. Some maternal sense to
stay, while Aunt Camille and Edna
split Adam and followed Eve

to a new religion, the one with
nirvana, where they let you out the loop
if you bitch loud enough. That's what
Florence taught us—if you squeal
again and again and again they
let you go. Let you unname and go
back to the time before blame.
Before they marked you woman
when you could just be, waist-deep
in your garden, running around
the Gulf naked, eating whatever
the fuck you want.

MANAGEMENT OF THE LIVING

El Caminito Del Rey, Spain

Here, they say Gal Gadot fell in love
with a donkey and demanded

it be delivered to her hotel room. The affinity for the wild is certainly
not new. Tippi Hedren played with lions
in her swimming pool. No one would rent her
the forty cats her film required, so she trained them
herself. They ate from her refrigerator. Watched TV with her daughter.
Always slept in her bed.

My lover tells me
to stop writing about wealthy women, and so I return
to my fieldnotes, determined to dig something of beauty from the canyons
filled with cave pigeons. I write, *What would any of us do*

if freed? and turn to the seeds

of the carob tree, so consistently shaped their weight was used
to measure gold. Pearls. Pepper. Bedouin shepherds fed their goats
on the same trees, infamously single-sex and finicky about flowering. My lover asks,
Where are you going with this?

and I return to my notes. My mother
pointed out that the flowers cloaking the Spanish mountains
are the pink ancestors of our oleanders. Poisonous, even to touch, but coveted
for their tenacity. Voila, my love: the act of flowering.

The root of *Florida, flora.* I remember
how our lemon trees bloomed most brilliantly post-hurricane.
Is this how I return to beauty?

Just go back
to the lions, says my lover now, but it was really the birds

that got Tippi. Hitchcock assured her they would all be
mechanical, but the prop men wore thick leather gloves
and tossed the gulls, ravens, and crows at her face

until one pierced her cheek and she collapsed. This was long before
the lions, but it never did stop. The leopards, cheetahs, tigers. The menagerie
of teeth, she kept at her command.

FIELDNOTES ON CAPE SAN BLAS

In a place named for the *Saint
of Wild Beasts*, a hurricane, too,
can make a house—a belly of
beams. A driftwood couch. A
real chandelier turned upside
down as a tree we adorned with
periwinkles & lion's paw & heart
shaped cockles to welcome the
sandpipers beneath our tarp
stretched bluer than sky, turning
its occupants marine inside.
Knowing no one had ever
come looking, we learned how
to make a house of our ruin.

AUGURIES BY MOUTH

The sign in my dentist's office promises x-rays are safer than eating

a banana, or living in a brick house, and we're in luck. There is less radiation

at sea level. See, how my tongue is split right along

the low country? Back home, our islands have secret horses,

and your inability to ride a horse is for the better: they are wild

and starving. Some say they should be euthanized for lack of

food, fresh water, veterinary care, but neglect keeps them

controlled. Beautiful, with distance. No bridge dissects

the Cumberland Sound and, no, you do not know how to swim, but

we've been over this—I'll teach you, again, and if you cannot learn,

I'll hold you in the shallow water by your ears so your body

floats in front of me. Lily-like. Amphibious. Able

to stay calm though I know the quickest way to learn

is thrash and swallow. My mother recalls hanging on

to the tail of the horse as it pulled her through the water. I, too, learned

to avoid the hooves. Grip the fetlock. Slip a metal bit between teeth

without struggle. Do you remember? Once, we went back

to the city, and when you asked me to trim your beard

in the shower, I lifted your lip and saw

the rot. The taste of pennies when I kissed you.

EKPHRASIS

nudity requires turpentine stillness, as art

students once laid their hands
to my shape : no bed, just a table
shivering with my weight
as fluorescent heads
aimed inward

to clean my body
of the forest falling
in ribbons through the windows : what felt small

in the high-ceiling
of their mouths became softer

and harder to cling to in fingertips :

like the sculpture I once turned to flour
with my own hands : de-limbing the plaster body
the hour before the show

knowing it didn't deserve
an afterlife : its rusted ribs were stolen
from the junkyard and the red berries
that spilled from its chest were

plastic : what did I desire?
I let a dozen strangers

rub their own what-ifs into
the body they were nostalgic

to lay their hands upon : the charcoal dimension

of moon-shivered hips or the ratio of scar
to long ankle : my mother

remembering how small and blue I began :
you know a thousand strangers could see you
naked?

what feels small

is this new house : blue and lacking any legs
or arm rests—no table, much less

a bed : in this hollow home, my ex-lover and I lay

skin-first on the carpet, my coat for a pillow :
every inch of what could burn : this house
does not belong to me though it could

have, he insists : an extra room for my studio and I could choose
the color of the kitchen, the thrill of hardwood
where we fan : in his language char :

the blue china quilt and divide the cold
dinner : no pots or pans to warm :

what's left of a body?

all the rooms are empty

including my lover, turning blue as the night
mutes every color : numbs even the red berries that soak

the carpet : there is no turpentine to cleanse

or burn : the forest I wish
would fall through the window and give innards
to this house instead of leaving

my body in ribbons : I say

we paint the bedroom to match the char
coal trapped beneath my nails but

there is no bed : no table : I lie absolutely
still as I am licked clean
by the moon, the wide paper mouth

shivering nothing but pigeons as
I coo
into my coat, coaxing any shadow
to bisect this fluorescent

still-life : my body

a bowl of grapes : my body

spilling from this white sheet : my body

has no part in this
as my blue love reaches for
what's left

and a thousand strangers
lay their hands upon me

FIELDNOTES ON CARRYING

Raise your ankles, my mother
warned as she pushed me
into the thousands of sting-
rays fleeing South, wings of
cartilage thumped my bright
yellow tube like a timpani.
The thinnest membrane
holds a body out of reach.
Children who learn to shuffle
their feet when entering high
tide are left unsure of how to
float, or why the Yucatán
calls the stingrays home.
How far did they carry me?
I knew my mother could not
have reached me without
a thousand holes herself.

DRIVING THROUGH DUNEDIN

It's November. My grandmother has died and left me
the malachite ring her husband gave to her
                                    before he died. Young. I am in love
with how the size of it gaudies the blue-green that would otherwise
be timeless. Adam and Eve must have loved each other very much

                                    with no other choice. Here, in Florida
          where my mother was born,
                    no mailbox a simple mailbox:
                    A mermaid, from seashells and a doll head.
                    A sea turtle, from fake leather and googly eyes.

The flamingos have faded from plastic pink to bone, but
                                    there are jellyfish in the trees
dripping Christmas lights. The whole canopy blinks technicolor, thanks to Max
who scours estate sales for their opulent frames, then sells them to neighbors cheap.

My mother is driving me to the trailer park where she grew up.
                    They're not trailers, they're mobile homes. She swears

it used to be beautiful; the grass was so thick
you could sink. *My dad planted only Saint Augustine. I stood there and watered it with the hose.*

          She tells me flamingos were once considered elegant.
          They were always sold in pairs: one looking up, one down.
                                    Mother-daughter.
                                    Husband-wife.

                                    I find the smell of sulfur soothing
as we pass the graveyard of shoes, visible in low tide.
The emerald ebb recedes and the mud spits them back

                                    in the same spot. This is Florida,
          where I was born and my mother has buried both parents.

Malachite is not expensive. Easy to carve and common
in dishware, but few rocks are so brilliantly green.

Can we drive down the street with the jellyfish?
Look closer, she says. *They're chandeliers.*

PART II

PARLOR TRICKS

NOTES ON DEVOTION

A man by the name of Skinner becomes famous
for keeping caged
                              pigeons, whom his clock feeds or starves
                              at random. Their tiny twitching heads exaggerate until

            one bird swings its weight like a pendulum;
            one turns counterclockwise three times;
            one aims its beak to the corner and sings, *My love*

let me break, which has nothing to do with the cage.
        The point is, the pigeons

                        invented their own religion. Aimed litanies
                                          at an empty sky until something
                        broke, and something

was mechanical.
I still hold the shape of his skull to my sleeping chest
                              and call his name
            over and over
to the wrong man. Though the manna that fell was nothing

        but accident, it conditioned the birds to aim weapons.
        The accuracy with which they pecked the homing radar

            was unswayed by Skinner's pistols
    or pressure chambers—the centrifugal loop that swung their bird-bones
                              broken, until their hearts

were locked in place.
If you feel pressure on the neck, remember—lockets

        used to be a sign of mourning, stuffed
with hair or cutouts of a lover's eyes. I've seen love

pecked to death and the gods
sculpted from that accident. I've aimed
my head to the corners of the sky and opened
my mouth so wide, I've thought
my beak would break. Like clockwork
I coo

Let me break

my love, and skin the feathers
from that wound. Religion requires ritual:
to do the same thing over
and over

despite pressure in the skull, or a pistol to the breast, but I still remember

my own young Sunday. The hollow sanctuary, where behind the preacher's head
a bird flew into the window over
and over, and we
just kept singing.

THE BATHTUB

On hurricane days, Mama dressed us

in life jackets and bike helmets and tucked us

in the bathtub. We swirled prophecies

of hair around the drain, soothsaying the rain

by the pink of the water line, as Mama split

her palms between all six ears

and softened the linoleum with psalms,

even the ones we want to forget. *Blessed is he*

that dasheth thy little ones on the rocks. The echoes

folded into a Book more believable than brimstone.

After all—swamps don't catch fire and we are a people

of Genesis. Our second-lines stomping

two-by-two through the Flood, with faith

our johnboats can hold each of us and the family

dog. Above us, the dove

or more likely the heron, circles

the swells until subsumed by salt, her babies

still tucked in the bulrush. Or babies

flown North to safety as the Atlantic

spins carnivorously counterclockwise.

One Christmas, I came home with a man

from New York who didn't know how to swim,

and Mama gave him a life jacket to keep in his Camry

just in case. My sisters laughed, and we all

moved North to drier land where no one

needs a johnboat. Where we can pretend

creation purls clockwise, and more time

is all we need—but when I see the rainbow

on TV reverse our blue-green swamps

to yellow-orange-red-black, I know

it will end with Mama

in her helmet, alone

in the bathtub, holding

her little dog.

IF WE MOVE BACK IN TOGETHER

we can't go back to New Orleans.
        The lights have been swallowed downriver

           and our apartment with the leaky window and
        my red Persian rugs would never
           float. But I know a place back east—

where the limestone sucks the sea
into little demitasse, and the hyacinth sips the sun
      black. Underneath,
        we could find

           a nice cave!

        And this time I'd let you choose
that Palladian Blue. Brawling over wallpaper
     is nothing compared to losing

              our own pigment.
          Our eyes.

      Things are different here!

        We have no way of knowing
    if our shapes grow globular
or melon-headed, tilting
      into the tarry depths. We become

          less aggressive. Languished by a lack
     of oxygen, no luxury
        of duvet. Feather for feather
            for eye.

      For eye.

                                        Our intimacy exquisitely

         alien to the surface creatures: we, circling
counterclockwise, mouths puckered
         to the gypsum walls. When I say,

                         You're not leaving this room

         until you have nothing left
to hide, your skin turns translucent
                 and you confess

                 each organ, in the violet technique
         of soft tissue.
         They say adaptation

         is more fluke than finesse, and unlikely
to favor us both but
                 this time, I see

                                 a white flash!

         means the legged creatures have come to
record our evolution. Don't listen

                                 if you hear them say *trapped.*

         The rules are different here.
                         Here—

                 I produce my own light
         and hold it on my tongue
until you follow it,
                 down.

FIELDNOTES ON HYDRANGEAS

Blue is a sign of acidity in the soil. My lover
from Queens hears not soil, but *soul*.
My slower tongue shows him what to bury:
pennies or rusted nails or lemon rind.
Control is a delicate science. I try to
convince him pH does not indicate
pollution, but I'm not so sure. Geophagy
is the practice of eating dirt. Women
in Georgia are known for their gardens.

INTERVIEW WITH A CERVIDOLOGIST

Technically, they are ungulates—
tender in-between the split hoof.

Their insides are torn
into chambers. Things grown
and digested in the dark.

Ever seen a deer eat a baby bird?
Feathers and all. They hunt
them down and strike
with hooves.

There's a natural order: *Ungulate.*
Ruminant. Cervid. Antlers

are just vascular velvet
that swells, turns mineral,
dies. Deer don't *have* to

break them off each year,
but you'd be surprised
how many creatures
choose desire.

We've done experiments

to stop deer from throwing their bodies
in front of cars. Do they really?

We lined the road with lights
to warn them. And it worked?

When it didn't, we covered them
with white sheets. The deer? The sheets

kept the deer away. Some strange
accident. You know, water deer

have fangs instead of antlers.
Even the women. But do they really

kill? It's all an art, this mounting
on the wall. Counting

our own small sins grown
in the dark. Like I said,

the deer threw their bodies
in front of me. *Life*

is no longer based on ability
to live outside the womb.

Life is now an object
of state protection. We track deer

according to the rose petal theory,
which means daughters

follow their mothers
in pink furrows, unfolding

in ways that can be violent. Homicide

begins with the heartbeat,
but do the mothers really kill

themselves? Let me ask
what you think of your own

thicket. How it holds the meadow
closed. Hides the precious
and dappled. There's a natural order.

Undulate. Cervix. I told you

we're more interested in wolves—
Freud was onto something

when he compared the deer stand
to a womb. A quiet muzzle pointed
from the inside out.

ETYMOLOGY OF CHLOROPHYLL

If fingernails could dig you like lichen
from my lexicon. In illness, I lop what is left
of you from my tongue, knowing to eliminate
is to loiter and loiter is in the same language

as love. As laceration. As love. We both used to

say as much though I admit at first
I pretended not to. I love—you lyre?
I love—you lick? I love—you
limp and lily-dark, you lovely
lump. Lewd as lamb. You say I was a lark

laid warm by my wingbones to your chest.
What do you expect? From this angle
a beak can do nothing but say, and certain languages

are sharpest dangled by the roots. Love,
from Germanic *lufu*, is intestinal and milky
like undug onions squeezed from mothers.
Love is not Latin, poised for markets smooth
and sellable. If we did love

in a soothe and soluble way,
we'd say *amor*—as in *enamored*,
or *unarmored*. Or maybe *phil*—as in
*I philosophize you. Philander you. Phillet you, my lovely
philodendron.* In another language I would let

my leaves grow leggy and long. Languish
on your windowsill without returning
any kind of sun. What word can tolerate
roots umbilically long?

In the language of philodendrons, there is
no word for *Lupus*. So I, philodendron,
cannot say this to you. Diagnoses
are intimately designed for a future,
and philodendrons speak only in present

tense, as I tuck what's left of my tongue
into teeth. *Lupus*, like scissors.
Lupus, like a loose leaf. When you call
for no other reason than to hear

what the doctor said: I lyre, I lick, I limp
lily-green, and leave you

phil as in *chlorophyll*, is all.

PATIENTS REGAIN SONG BEFORE SPEECH

So many lengths of catgut can be strung

from a body. Each body could contain hundreds

of orchestras, Mozart insists against my grandmother's skin.

I believe some part of her body still vibrates

beneath all its soft battles and sinews, and Mozart

understands. He is praised for the silence

between his notes. No one knows the reason

for his untimely death, if you can call death

a simple matter of bones, not the thick oil of memory left

on the fridge handle, the kitchen window

where she smashed the gnats. My grandmother

never learned to cook, but she filled her kitchen with hundreds

of roosters, perched in wait for the day she could break

their ceramic silence. Battalions arranged in the bellies

of unused appliances, or riding the spine

of the keyboard I never saw her play. She loved the button

that looped *Eine kleine Nachtmusik* through plastic speakers.

We loved to pound our own melodies over Mozart's

masterpiece, over her stories. I don't know who to blame

for the silence, so I sing. Can you hear me, Mema?

Mozart is the only one who understands.

Over take-out subs and tins of butter cookies, I hope

he is scribbling down your stories, and when his quill

strikes the words you are trying to speak,

I hope the rooster he plucked it from screams wildly.

IF WE STAGE THE WIZARD OF OZ WITH ALLIGATORS

We have to go *big* or go home—dilate the tornado

    with saltwater. Re-name it Hurricane Matthew, or Ike—the name

is unimportant, just make it bigger than anyone's seen.

    In this scene, twist Dorothy's dress into a heavy tail—roll!

        The death roll—rumbling over the rain—ho!

      She snags a couple fish. Let her eat,

    like they wouldn't let Judy, and let the rain sweep

the whole scene technicolor. Re-plant Dorothy in a peanut field and

    don't let the farmer shoot Toto—Dorothy scoops him in her mouth

like a tender mother, says the herpetologist on set, who insists

    a witch can live for 80 million years, but in winter

her reflexes dull. Too slow to skirt the house—the tree—which falls

    at the nape of her skull.

        The wicked witch! The wicked witch!

    Ding dong,

Dorothy steals her teeth.

      Dorothy is washed out to sea

    and hungry—the beaches bared of lions

    and the sea-crows sunk with oil—

        oh my!

    The good witch crawls from the sewer, and something ruby

slips down her throat. There's no place like

    the Emerald Coast, but the homing instincts of gators

break down after 60 miles. Dorothy must find her way

    to the Wonderful Wizard who cries: *Pay no attention!*

And demands proof of melting.

The Wizard says: *Click your teeth three times—*

there's no place like home,

there's no place like home,

there's no place like home anymore.

Anymore. But keep this part the same: make the Wizard a man—

with a human hand—

to yank the curtain over his eyes.

Circled by gators and Dorothy

with twice the teeth.

So when the lizards of Oz ask who's to blame

for their bayous boiling—swamp fires roiling—storms

that drag them to Texas or trees that snap

on their necks—consult the herpetologist on set who says:

There is no such thing as a feeding frenzy.

Gators are coordinated

when they face the current.

Arrange their jaws side by side

so not one human escapes.

FIELDNOTES ON JUNIPER

I am always looking for proof. There
in the canyons of El Chorro, the guide
pointed to the mountain that once
cupped an ocean in its peak. The sea floor
stayed put even as fresh rivers carved
around it, pushing octopus and urchin
toward the sun. We know this now,
the guide said, for the juniper that grows
along the lips. Not the skeletons:
the unlucky fish who felt the moon
lose her grip on the tides. Who carved
their shapes in the rock before anyone
could name them. There are planets
whose own gravity consumes them, and
plants I call in Latin for the softness
of rhyme. Here: I will say them right.
Snakeroot. Slashpine. Love-lies-bleeding.

THE SARGASSUM FISH

Our desire to call it Emerald
is a hoax. By June, the waves
are so thick with seaweed you can hardly raise your head. It was a game
for my sisters & I

to lift the curly clumps and seize the sargassum fish before they darted
to new hiding. Tiny bodies changing color
in our palms—mottled gold to dark.
It's my mother's fault:

my eyes should have been green, like my sisters.
My aunts. My grandmother never became a wife
but still gave her children his name. *Blue*. Desire

means every woman to run has kept close to the coast.
I am looking up the name

of Lot's wife when I find *Wives of the Antediluvian Patriarchs:*
Emzara, Noah's wife.
Awan, Eve's first daughter.
Edna, wife to Methuselah. Then again, to Enoch. Nothing is certain

but *Wives of Before-the-Flood* is a name you can only give
too late. During a storm surge, the safest place to swim

is far beyond the breakpoint, but as I said, the waves are too heavy
to clear with two hands. Pried apart, you can see

the biggest threat to the sargassum fish is its own kin:

One was dissected and found with sixteen juveniles in its stomach.

MY ANCESTORS IN SOUTH CAROLINA

In New Orleans, I watch
a man walk backwards
around the clot in St. Charles
where they removed
General Lee. His pedestal still staked
like a clock dial in the heart
of the roundabout. An hour hand
could sweep the man's feet right out from his
body if he weren't facing counterclockwise.
In Madagascar, they believe time faces
backwards: the past fans out before you,
while the future prickles dark at your spine.
If so, a hundred and seventy years ahead,
South Carolina secedes in our dining room,
so goes the family myth. If I could climb
my father's shoulders, I would see the signatures
scrape our kitchen table. More clearly if my ancestors
would tilt the table in my direction, or
even better if someone flipped it altogether
and sent the ink spattering into a nobler
family myth: *Your black curls sprung when your grand-*
father smashed the inkwell. Your green eyes shattered
with that glass. In Madagascar, you can't turn away from
your ancestors, or your ghost will be left to wander.
I wonder how far South Carolina stands
from New Orleans, from the unnamed
location where they hid General Lee. If
his new tower is taller than the barren
plinth that pins the roundabout to this era.
How long has his hair grown? How many
tug his beard? *Bobby Lee, Bobby Lee,*
let down your heirs. How many ghosts
at kitchen tables will never have to wander.
My grandma said to keep a guest
from returning, you should sweep as soon
as they leave. The myths we foretell
are prettier than what fans before our
faces. The past still fobbed to our
breasts. Our ancestors carve their names
in our kitchen tables and urge us
to eat, but no matter how far I wander,
the clock hand sweeps
my feet from beneath me
and stakes
its dark dial
in my back.

FIELDNOTES ON THE BLOODMOON

After three days, my blood is still thin and
bright as moon when it gathers in my
thumbnail—the odd finger for digging the
soft cup from my cervix. It makes sense
as ceremony: your plane lurches from
LaGuardia like a stork from a hot stove
coil. What goes looking still for heat? I
refuse to believe the red speckling the tile
is translucent and early for the sake of
a pill meant to keep small mouths from
opening. We agreed. I'll write no more
poems about birds, or anything that has
learned to bleed, or that which must do so
to know the weight of its leaving.

ERESHKIGAL, OUR SINKHOLE SISTER

the Floridian earth   has as many mouths as   stars imploding
we planted   houses   in the center
smack on the lips of   a goddess   we never name
Hecate   Nepthys   Innana
some gods   we borrow   but Ereshkigal will
take   her own sister   ring by robe
by limb   she bids   her sister
remember   she is animal   no different than
how they played   horses   in the backyard.
how they pretended to be   birds   naked. whole lakes.
whole   mouths   can swallow
and regurgitate   whole sisters   overnight. *ready or not*
here I   *come*   Ereshkigal makes us
remember   to be   symbiotic:
to align   bodies   with limestone lines
limestone with bodies   in the backyard   see
our sister   the size of a saucer
opens   her arms ready
to swallow.

LOVE POEM FOR MY BIRD DOG

I wanted to write a love poem, but it ended up
about my bird dog who wouldn't hunt. Who only chased shadows

round and round the back field until we had to
tie him up. Then one day, he offered up

a mouth full of bird. I wanted to write
about the bird, but this is a love poem—

or it could have been if I wrote about
my yellow dog, who once bit my neighbor so badly

the police took her away for a month and my bird dog
stopped running circles. Stopped eating. Went blind

with missing her, despite the fact that yellow dog
never liked him, or even noticed when he died.

But this was meant to be a love poem, so maybe I should write
about my black horse, Daizy Mae, who was tall and fast and mean

to everyone but Sunny, the red horse who never left her side.
Never bit or kicked or broke down the fence to run

into the road unless she was following Daizy.
She was following Daizy when she climbed from the ditch

onto the highway, but being sweet and slow and
loyal, could not leap from the blacktop in time.

We found Daizy after the accident
down the road, chewing grass, unbothered.

Let me try again. The black horse. The red horse.
The dogs. Perhaps I will write this poem

to the bird I pulled from my dog's mouth.
How I wrapped it in a washrag and laid it

in a shoebox, tapping its small chest for hours until
I had to accept it was dead. How I dug

a tiny grave, but when I reached for the body
it was gone. Maybe I am writing to the shadow

of the bird that my dog who wouldn't hunt chased
again across the field. You, yes you—I need you

to know I would have kept you, and loved you
most, had you never escaped my hands.

PART III

HYPOTHETICAL MOONS

MOON SONG FOR MY MOTHER

My mother says my troubles started
               with the moon. As a child, I insisted on sleeping on the roof
                            where the bright crash
of waves invaded the nylon cocoon
she zipped over my head. She always warned
I wouldn't sleep, just like she warned ballet
               would break all the small bones in my feet.
               My mother and I wear the same narrow nine.

     After each foot surgery she woke screaming of alligators
                        who wouldn't let go
of her pinky toe. *You can't inherit all the bad things*
               from me, but it's true—

I never sleep. I listen to recordings of humpback whales and arrange my pillow

so I can pretend the sound of traffic is the pines. They too
sing complex lullabies: rumbling, honking, the occasional crash of metal.

                 In this house, I have an excuse—an animal
        rattled my ceiling all night long
until my landlord installed a small white box. Now all I hear is
                          tick, tick, tick

and still, I cannot sleep. Scientists have mapped whale songs
     onto musical staffs and determined they're all
               for love, but it's true—the whales are dying

of sound. Propellors & seismic airguns test for oil
     every ten seconds, for weeks on end—
                 love song, love song, love song.
                     I am scared

of how my mother's pills make her forget things after dark.
As a child, I begged her to sing me Old Rugged Cross before bed.
The one with the animals...
though they were never in the lyrics.
I made it up

she said, each time she woke screaming in the night. Tonight, I know she is awake
when she calls to say, *Look at the moon...*
I know she won't remember anything I say, so I say

the alligators have gone to sleep.
The whales are safe in their cocoons. Outside,
the pine trees tiptoe, mouths
pressed to the moon.

SEARCHING FOR AMELIA

When my grandpa found the humpback whale washed to shore, he reached

       for the barnacled lips as if to enter

right back into her sitting room. As if to brush the tongue, where

       he could still picture the famous aviatrix

sitting cross-legged, chin tilted to admire the hole above.

       I always wanted a skylight. The light falling

from the blowhole like moon gathering on her cheekbones, sharper

       than he'd seen in photographs.

Miles of ocean off Howland Island, dozens of Navy planes,

       and he had been the one to find her

in that most unlikely place, a tiny drainage tube taped to her nose. *The air needs a way*

       to escape. Portraits of her husband

were pinned, quivering along the soft palate, and she'd strung

       the baleen with blooms of seaweed, wilting

as houseplants do under tender fret. Every corner of her belly-home

       glittered in salty veneer, but the tongue

was most luxurious, its high pile plush cleansed carefully of lingering krill.

       My grandpa said she'd perched

on the fatty muscle like an equestrian, hands straddled for balance,

       hovering briefly each time the whale breached.

He'd tried to blame the rise and swell of his stomach on seasickness,

       but really was unable to turn away

from her pale ropy wrists. The holly glow of her hair. Unable to do anything

       but ask, *How did you get here?*

to which she replied, *It's less biblical than it looks.* Staring into the eyes

       he'd heard should be blue. *Come back with me,*

he wanted to say but only offered to tie her Oxford shoes

and would have—had aluminum

not been strewn around the room. Remains of the wings shredding any hope

of tenderness. Instead, he asked, *Don't you miss the sky?*

But she was admiring how her face multiplied in all the twisted metal.

The possibilities they revealed. Here,

the only use for propellors was to flense an animal's fat.

Because fat makes you float

to the surface, she laughed. *And who would want that?*

FIELDNOTES ON THE RED-BELLIED WOODPECKER

First, the downy woodpecker my new love
found lying on the sidewalk. He did not recount
to me the teethmarks until we'd driven away,
and I could not say if I'd rather see one dead
or not at all. The birds here are foreign
to me, and I could only imagine it by its
name, all pillowy ruff & baby fat. I think of it
later, watching the next bird hammer the dead
tree outside the bedroom window as I straddle
his bare waist, kiss his silvering temples. His
eyes are closed as I take note of the rippled
wings, the scarlet scalp, these parts of the body
I save for him, so later he can help me name it.

THE WOMEN OF WEEKI WACHEE

I have seen the shows:

women

behind glass with cheeks artificially
neon, fish tails practiced to resist the jerk

of drowning. The plastic tubes
they hold to their lips. I know the stories—real life sirens

but for the silence
of a language they made themselves: hand signals warn
of alligators. Moccasins. Motorcars
they run to flag down. This vocabulary of *escape*

I learned from my mother—the parlor tricks
of her body. First baby born blue. A plastic tube

taped to my lips. My mother assures—no one is looking
as we open our necks
in the brightest colors, fan gills

along faulty tissue. Mermaid stories
are never gentle. Ancient. *You know, some women would kill*

to bend like this. She promises: no one is looking

for a cure.
But really, some women would kill—

SEARCHING FOR AMELIA

In adapting to her watery home, Amelia learned

       that even more useless than planes

were seahorses; terrible swimmers, they refused to be tied

       in her hands. But she was amused

by how the males carried the babies—so, could my grandpa

       carry her babies?

Back to her darling George, with an apology

       for skipping their honeymoon.

For instead taking a tour with Beech-Nut Chewing Gum

       and bringing home a suitcase full

of sticky souvenirs. Surely by now George had chewed through the bulk, pacing

       their once-shared sitting room, awaiting

her improbable return. Perhaps swallowing bits of lumpy yellow grief

       or fingering their wet accumulation

on the coffee table, shaping until it began to look more and more

       like her. Until it called to him

in the grim hours of the night, *You forgot my nose, darling! Have another piece.*

       Pretty soon I will pace this room

with you again. My grandpa wanted to kiss George almost as badly

       as he wanted to kiss Amelia, if only to share

his heartbreak with someone who understood. Which left the question:

       What could he carry back?

Amelia had lined the pink wall with bundles of her scaly

       metamorphoses—a collection of young

unsmiling and silent, as if unsure of where their mouths

       should split or tails should fall.

She admired the offspring before adding kindly, *Perhaps give a few to my dear*

Charles Lindbergh, to replace what he found

in the woods. The cries he wished he had heard. She offered, too, her shoe size—

a narrow nine—so her children would know

how tall to grow. He could give them the pocket-sized portrait of his own that he kept

in his cockpit, so they would understand

why Charles had nicknamed her *Lady Lindy*. Their same shy mouths, the gray dapple

in their eyes. *But how?*

She explained: in times of desperation, some species can spawn

their own replicates, life

pulled from impossible hollows—though this is mostly observed

in invertebrates. She offered

her own spine as souvenir, but my grandpa accepted only

her hand. He begged, actually,

for something to remember. He'd been searching so long. Always wanting

children of his own to teach about

seahorses; to share the joy of the metal detector chirping along the sandbar; to point

at the green edge of the sea, sinking

into the sun and ask, *Where does it go after this?*

PARLOR TRICKS

were part of the diagnosis.
When you were young
did you ever perform

strange feats
for friends and family?

I grab the metal railing.
Lower myself

into the springs
where the water is

glowing!
Radium

is a natural element.
Did you ever perform—

My mother
can bend her legs behind her ears

and hold her breath
for five minutes.
She taught me to swim

in these pools, famous
for the women who flicker

plastic fish tails underwater.
Can you think back—
my grandmother

was a dancer, too.
My sisters. My aunts.

It is more common in women.
I pretend to be water

proof, prehistoric
in the way I slide

through my skin, slinking apart
at the sockets.

Will it progress?
My mother assured:
the half-life of radium

can take
a thousand years.
Connective tissue

is the unstable element.
The doctor repeats:
Parlor tricks

are the first element
of diagnosis—like

this? I open
my shoulder
blades and dig

for my mother's
bones. Each one
luminescent.

FIELDNOTES ON RED

He tells me about the old language,
in which this color was a synonym
for beauty. I tell him we are not too
far removed from loons, who are
not too far from penguins, and I
too require a Petoskey stone as
proposal. He combs the beach, his
middle finger still wet and, in Old
Slavic, beautiful, from the lip
of the ginger bottle he broke
open, for me. Inside, something
turns to ruin. He recites Pushkin,
You & You. We are supposed to go
dancing in the park, when a friend
calls: none of the women arrived,
and it is just five men waiting in the
cold. Someone jokes about what
Siberian wives will do for their
husbands, and we take our time.
Lean our bodies over the bridge to
watch the salmon nose the current,
the long-bodied females that flash
their   bellies   in   the   sun.

THE BIOLUMINESCENT BAYS OF VIEQUES

No, I have never seen the bioluminescent bays of Vieques.

We're in company, so I cannot protest
when my lover again tells the story of how the fisherman

pulled the tarp over their small boat. How he and his then-
lover splashed their hands in the waves tracing trails

of light. He explains, again, how the color changes
from person to person, but I've found no proof.

The internet says the deeper you go, the more green
the monsters. Always, the exceptions:

Dragonfish turn red. Octopi, yellow.
The real plural of *octopus* is just

octopus, but we make the same aberration
of *hippopotami*. I fear the same mistakes

haunt us in every life. My lover claims he saw white.
She, blue. The small space we now call ours is harrowed still

by matching coffee mugs and the pink deodorant
I wouldn't let him toss. The feathery handcuffs I snapped

the first time he tied me up. I promised
a love poem, but it has turned again

to this: the anglerfish attracts its mate
and prey with the same lure, is the best theory we've got.

I have nightmares each time I fall in love,
and no one can tell me why. One friend suggested

another body makes the bed safe enough
to confront the darkness. Another suggested

I invent the monsters. A matter of balance.
Imagine what you will

of those depths, but humans too
are bioluminescent. The glimmer,

too faint for the naked eye, is brightest
around the neck, cheeks in late afternoon.

I think of the last time I saw my ex. We drove
to the darkest corner of the state, a rocky coastline swarmed

with couples. I assumed them all in love, except us, undercover
as the night scooped each body into hiding.

I couldn't tell if my eyes were open
when the towers of Northern Lights

besieged our jetty. I sent my mother pictures
of their blue-violet bounds, but in person

they were white. It is hard to regret beauty and easy
to lie. We both have ex-lovers, of the other,

we despise, though there is nothing in him to blame.
He loves with translucence. A goodness that washes

each pink hour of our days. As he goes on, still,
about the bays, I think of how algal blooms cause

skin infections, death.
I have stories I keep to myself—

on a moonless night in Madagascar,
the worms in the well water waited to flash

blue until the moment the cup touched my lips. In that half-second,
I swallowed. Not all darkness feels the same.

Sometimes he pulls the sheets over our heads and navigates
the salty waves of my body, his beard scrubbing

my last soft skin as if he forgives
the alien thing rooted inside me, or remembers me

young, on the night beaches of Georgia, running my hand
along the surf so the warm sand sparkled with friction.

No, I have never seen
the bioluminescent bays of Vieques, but I know

the story: how the fisherman pulled the tarp
over their heads. How he splashed

his hands in the waves, and made the darkness
turn to light.

FIELDNOTES ON HYPOTHETICAL MOONS

The existence of Saturn's rings
required a fantastic collision of
moons: one survivor, and one
that shattered into a million
smaller versions of itself. Most
moons are named for Greek
gods, but this one we called
Chrysalis, for butterflies. Millions
of monarchs crossed our beaches
each October. Our fingertips
shone orange from grasping.

SEARCHING FOR AMELIA

My grandpa was loyal. He never revealed

that the children weren't his. He would have followed her right

through the end, if not for those green eyes

he had to carry across the sea. Back to the little house he built

under the orange trees

and the yard he filled with salvaged metal.

He was devoted

to melding the scraps into toys, to building his collection of telescopes. Ceramic

figurines. Bobby pins. Bones, including the bundle

he kept by his bed. The thirteen he claimed added up to one finger, minus the tip.

This was her. Reports claim

that the island he searched was pocked with giant crab feet, reef shark teeth,

but nothing more. No footprints circling the remains

of a campfire. Some dead birds. A turtle. A rubber sole stamped *Cat Paw Company,*

size nine. Not even

the forensically-trained-bone-sniffing-border-collies could find

a sign of life beneath the ren tree, but

when the humpback washed to shore, my grandpa laid his hand to the pleats

of its upturned chin and flinched—nothing

makes you jump like the song of what you thought

was dead. The brief harmony

of their cries obscured each other, but even then

he couldn't step away

from the heave of its belly—the plastic knotted around its fluke

precisely, with care, as if he himself

could have dragged the beast to shore. Pulled from its throat the uvula

chandelier, carved open the skylight

for which my grandmother begged when they married; the bay window he built so

        she could watch the hummingbirds gather

in the arms of her favorite fig tree, beneath which she left nightly bowls

        of kibble for the creatures

she called cats. Their eyes shining green as they left small gifts

        along the roots. Half-warm and chewed.

Her own air escaping the tiny tube on her cheek. In times

        of health, my grandmother

buried each gift in small boxes along the beach, and when the cats died,

        she buried them, too. The raccoons,

the possums, the unnamable hands that my grandpa later

        unearthed, folding them

in a baby blanket next to his pillow, claiming, *I loved you*

        like my own.

ELK LAKE

There is no horizon
between the night sky and the edge of this lake, named for its abundance
    of an animal that within a decade of naming

was hunted extinct. I speak too much of apocalypse

        says my new love, to whom I cannot admit
          the rings of Saturn
    are disappearing. Its gravity overwhelms the tiny moons fighting
    to keep the bands in place. As we witness

            the citrine body from the midnight dock,
    I say instead how one ring wavers so precisely
        it makes music
we could record on sheets. Doing so would reveal what lies

at the inner core, but there are more important endeavors.
We have begun, before bed, singing silly love songs
until guitar strings slice his fingertips and he apologizes
        for the softness. He makes me
    tomato soup & grilled cheese while I shower and then
joins me. Kisses my knees, my fingertips. Every body part we dipped in the lake
    burns, and I explain

    how on Saturn, the rings are made of ice—some grains as small as sugar, some as
    wide as a house. And what if we do? Make a house of our love, with a garden

of tomatoes, spicy arugula. Orchards of stone fruit & an abundance
of choke cherry to sustain the little herd of elk that's been reintroduced. Time
    means nothing against efforts of love.
        We still have 100 million years
before Saturn loses its rings, but mere centuries since Galileo

first found the planet in his telescope and mistook the rings for ears.
I understand this desire, I do.

To hold a face between my hands and call it golden.

THE LOON'S SOLID BONES HELP HER SINK

My mother wants to buy a house in the mountains where her mother
lived. I want to celebrate Saturnalia instead of Christmas. Midwinter,
I wax the horsehair of my grandmother's psaltery, last re-stretched
the day I was born. She believed in the gods I am searching for. Saturn

is the god of time :
generation : dissolution. I assume his occupation marine, but
Wikipedia says *satus* : to sow, *stercus* : manure. In the ruin of Pompeii,
he was painted sickle in hand, veiled in white, waiting for the world
to green. What dissolves time

more absolutely than love?
The Appalachian Mountains will outlive the rings of Saturn. Already
more ancient than the moons that shattered in its orbit. Already older
than bones : consider, the first fish, jawless and tailed, walled into the
softness of its song

throat-first. My lover
holds me at the edge of the evening lake where we watch the loon
dive again, again. Despite her silence, he recognizes her by the length
of time she disappears, and I choose to believe him. All we know

we know from fossils
which are just cavities, occurring in one of two ways : decay or self-
dissolution. There were years my sisters and I pried seashells from
the garden and stuck river mica to our skin like scales. There is proof
that bone sacrifices itself to soft tissue

under pressure. My mother wants
to move to the mountains she never knew. My lover tells me
the loon will flee come winter. If not towards warmth, then salt.
This lake will freeze by the next new moon and

who am I to speak?

I know only the warm-weather creatures : the whale evolved back to the sea after it learned to walk. Now, the humpbacks sing as if standing upside down, noses pointed to the depths. You see, sirens were fated to death if a lover escaped their song. The drowning, a means of survival. I always believed them

half-fish, but they were really half-woman, half-bird : feathered like the loon with bones thick enough to plunge their low-slung bodies through the ice.

What is the opposite of dissolution? My mother abandons the mountains. Moves back to the coast in the middle of a hurricane. Marks the wall where the water will rise.

NOTES

The Elephant Mother

In 2021, Carol Buckley founded the Elephant Refuge North America in the cow fields of Attapulgus, GA. She was devoted to protecting the elephant Tarra, whom she met in 1974, but Tarra's presence at the refuge was unexpectedly preceded by Bo.

Widdershins

Douglas Kearney gifted this word to me over a lovely brunch in Ann Arbor, MI, in response to an earlier title for this collection.

Garden of Eve

From roughly 1953 to 1979, United States hurricanes and tropical storms were named after women. If a hurricane was particularly devastating, her name was retired.

Alice, Barbara, Carol, Dolly, Edna, and Florence were the first six named hurricanes. Carol has been re-named Camille in this poem, after Hurricane Camille in 1969.

Management of the Living

The Birds (1963) was one of many films in which Tippi Hedren experienced and spoke out about director Alfred Hitchcock's harrowing control and abuse. Hedren was unable to break her contract with Hitchcock for many years and therefore acted in many of his films against her will.

The title was inspired by Antoine Traisnel's book, *Capture: American Pursuits and the Making of a New Animal Condition*, in which he argues that the desire to "contain and record disappearing animals" in nineteenth-century literature corresponded to "the systemic disappearance of animals effected by unprecedented changes in the land, the rise of mass slaughter, and the new awareness of species extinction."

Driving Through Dunedin, FL

In Dunedin, Max Helms transforms discarded chandeliers into extravagant tree art. He makes and sells them cheaply "just to bring joy." Locals in Dunedin hang them in their yard, where they stay lit year-round.

Notes on Devotion

During World War II, B. F. Skinner worked on Project Pigeon for the United States government, training pigeons to guide missiles by pecking at the target. The experiments were designed to test the pigeons' resilience by firing pistols near their ears, placing them in pressure chambers, exposing them to bright flashes, etc.

In 1948, Skinner published "Superstition in the Pigeon," in which he claims the birds created their own individual rituals to receive food rewards and practiced them even when there was no real correlation between the ritual and the reward.

Interview with a Cervidologist

This poem borrows language from three sources. The first, an interview of zoologists Rhiannon Kirton & Rhiannon Jakopak, by Alie Ward on *Ologies*.

The second, Georgia House Bill 481, also known as the "Heartbeat Bill," which was passed in Georgia's General Assembly in 2019. This bill made abortion illegal after six weeks of pregnancy, except in cases of emergency, rape, or incest, which were made illegal after twenty weeks.

The third, a quote by hunter Shawn Perich in *Northern Wilds*: "Maybe Sigmund Freud, were he a deer hunter, would have an explanation. Perhaps, by going inside a dark box, the modern deer hunter reenters the womb."

If We Stage the Wizard of Oz with Alligators

This poem is based on the misfortunes of two unlucky alligators: In 2008, an alligator was swept into the Gulf of Mexico by Hurricane Ike and carried over 300 miles, from Johnson's Bayou, LA to Padre Island, TX. In 2016, an alligator was flattened by a falling tree during Hurricane Matthew on Wassaw Island, GA.

Information about these events comes from "Long-Distance Displacement of a Juvenile Alligator by Hurricane Ike" by Ruth M. Elsey and Chelsea Aldrich, as well as two *National Geographic* articles: "Alligator Crushed by Tree—Here's How It Happened," by Jason Bittel, and "Alligator 'Feeding Frenzy' Video Shows Teamwork" by Ker Than.

The Sargassum Fish

Observations of cannibalism in the sargassum fish are cited from "Nature's Fast Feeder: The Frogfish" in the 1981 issue of *Nassau Guardian*.

Ereshkigal, Our Sinkhole Sister

In Greek mythology, Hecate is associated with entryways, thresholds, sorcery, and necromancy. Ambivalent and liminal, she can traverse all realms: sky, earth, sea, and the underworld.

In Egyptian mythology, Nephthys was associated with death and burial, and possesses the ability to revive the dead. Her twin sister, Isis, is associated with birth and healing.

In Mesopotamian mythology, Ereshkigal was goddess of the underworld while her sister Innana was goddess of the heavens. In the myth *Inanna's Descent*, Inanna descends to the underworld to visit Ereshkigal. Ereshkigal orders that Inanna strip more clothing at each descending door. Upon her naked arrival, Ereshkigal murders her.

Searching for Amelia

This poem re-imagines the story of my great-grandmother and step-great-grandfather: Grandmommy and Grand. Grand participated in the naval search for Amelia Earhart in 1937.

Because I never knew them, I can only fill in the last chapter of their story with memories of my grandparents, Mema and G. Daddy. Both generations were marked by the devastation of dementia and the devotion of loving through that grief. Both generations also made the decision to choose family over truth.

Details of Amelia Earhart's possible survival and whereabouts are sourced from several theories, most significantly the discovery in 1991 on Nikumaroro Island: a shoe, a campfire, animal remains, and human bones.

The Women of Weeki Wachee and Parlor Tricks

The Weeki Wachee, whose name means "little spring" in the Seminole language, is a spring-fed river that glows due to its natural radium content. The Weeki Wachee mermaid shows, which began in 1947 and continue today, allow audiences to observe women through the glass of an underwater theater carved into the limestone. The women swim amongst the fish, manatees, and other wildlife that pass through the shows, including the occasional alligator.

First-hand accounts come from, Vicki Smith, "the world's oldest performing mermaid," who tells her story in "A Dip into Southern Mermaid History" in *Garden & Gun*.

ACKNOWLEDGMENTS

My deepest gratitude—

To Mama and Daddy for the leather journals and the loquat trees. To my sisters, Sarah Anne and Emily, for climbing those trees with me. To Mema, G. Daddy, and Fred, for your stories; and to Mimi, for reading everything I wrote. I miss you so much.

To my writing family in the Helen Zell Writers Program. To my eight-nation army: Abby, Bridgette, Matt, Robert, Austin, Dave, and Olivia, for your trespacity in these wet endeavors. To Maia, for your generous friendship. To Amanda, for your aquatic kinship. To the faculty: Linda Gregerson, Tung-Hui Hu, Sumita Chakraborty, and Khaled Mattawa, for showing me the depths of my own voice. To Abigail McFee, for countless exchanges of poems, puzzle-piecing of manuscripts, tarot card readings, half-births, and burials of our most precious parts.

To Joan Beers, Alan Michael Parker, and Katie St. Clair, for your belief in my beginnings. To the Anthropology faculty at Davidson College for valuing my voice as a poet.

To Miss Debbie and Taylor, for teaching me to talk to animals. To Leigh and India, for traversing womanhood with me. To Taranjit, for allowing me to wrestle our most vulnerable parts in these pages.

To my loved ones in Madagascar for showing me the expansiveness of family. For inviting me into your own worlds of poetry just as I was creating my own.

To my own little family. To Sarabi, for giving me purpose. To Steve, for all the days spent collecting Petoskey stones, oyster shells, and maple seeds to decorate our house of love. For all the days to come.

Finally, my gratitude to Maggie Smith for selecting this manuscript as winner for the Ballard Spahr Prize. To Bailey Hutchinson, Mary Austin Speaker, and everyone at Milkweed Editions for your kindness in the process of bringing this book to life. And to all the readers, editors, and judges who allowed these poems into the world first:

American Poetry Review: "Widdershins"

Bellevue Literary Review: "Etymology of Chlorophyll"

2022 John & Eileen Allman Prize for Poetry, judged by Phillip B. Williams

Beloit Poetry Review: "The Elephant Mother" & "Management of the Living"
2023 Adrienne Rich Award for Poetry Finalist, judged by Marie Howe

Cincinnati Review: "Notes on Devotion"
2022 Robert and Adele Schiff Award Winner, judged by Rebecca Lindenberg

Driftwood Press: "The Bathtub" and "Driving Through Dunedin"
2023 In-House Poetry Contest Winner

Malahat Review: "Interview with a Cervidologist"
2023 Open Season Award Winner, judged by Ki'en Debicki

Palette Poetry: "Elk Lake"
2022 Love & Eros Prize, 3rd Place, judged by Carl Phillips

PRISM International: "The Archaeology Magazine"
2021 Witness Literary Award Finalist, judged by Phillip B. Williams

San Diego Poetry Annual: "Moon Song for My Mother"
2023 Steve Kowit Poetry Prize, Second Runner-Up, judged by Kim Addonizio

An earlier version of this manuscript, titled *All the Little Beasts,* was awarded the 2022 Meader Family Award at the University of Michigan, judged by Kaveh Akbar, Diane Seuss, Victoria Chang and Airea D. Matthew.

CAROLINE HARPER NEW is a poet and artist from Bainbridge, Georgia, with a background in anthropology. She lived for several years in Madagascar and now holds an MFA from the University of Michigan. Her poetry has appeared in *American Poetry Review, Beloit Poetry Review, Cincinnati Review, Southern Humanities Review,* and elsewhere. She has received the *Palette Poetry* Love & Eros Prize, *Malahat Review* Open Season Award, *Cincinnati Review* Robert and Adele Schiff Award, and *Bellevue Literary Review* John & Eileen Allman Prize for Poetry. She lives in Ann Arbor, Michigan.

The twelfth award of

THE BALLARD SPAHR PRIZE FOR POETRY

is presented to

CAROLINE HARPER NEW

by
Milkweed Editions
and
The Ballard Spahr Foundation

First established in 2011 as the Lindquist & Vennum Prize for Poetry, the annual Ballard Spahr Prize for Poetry awards $10,000 and publication by Milkweed Editions to a poet residing in Minnesota, Iowa, Michigan, North Dakota, South Dakota, or Wisconsin. Finalists are selected from among all entrants by the editors of Milkweed Editions. The winning collection is selected annually by an independent judge. The 2022 Ballard Spahr Prize for Poetry was judged by Maggie Smith.

Milkweed Editions is one of the nation's leading independent publishers, with a mission to identify, nurture, and publish transformative literature, and build an engaged community around it. The Ballard Spahr Foundation was established by the national law firm of Ballard Sphar, LLC, and is a donor-advised fund of The Minneapolis Foundation.

milkweed
EDITIONS

Founded as a nonprofit organization in 1980, Milkweed Editions is an independent publisher. Our mission is to identify, nurture, and publish transformative literature, and build an engaged community around it.

Milkweed Editions is based in Bdé Óta Othúŋwe (Minneapolis) within Mní Sota Makhóčhe, the traditional homeland of the Dakhóta people. Residing here since time immemorial, Dakhóta people still call Mní Sota Makhóčhe home, with four federally recognized Dakhóta nations and many more Dakhóta people residing in what is now the state of Minnesota. Due to continued legacies of colonization, genocide, and forced removal, generations of Dakhóta people remain disenfranchised from their traditional homeland. Presently, Mní Sota Makhóčhe has become a refuge and home for many Indigenous nations and peoples, including seven federally recognized Ojibwe nations. We humbly encourage our readers to reflect upon the historical legacies held in the lands they occupy.

milkweed.org

Milkweed Editions, an independent nonprofit publisher, gratefully acknowledges sustaining support from our Board of Directors; the Alan B. Slifka Foundation and its president, Riva Ariella Ritvo-Slifka; the Amazon Literary Partnership; *Copper Nickel*; the McKnight Foundation; the National Endowment for the Arts; the National Poetry Series; and other generous contributions from foundations, corporations, and individuals. Also, this activity is made possible by the voters of Minnesota through a Minnesota State Arts Board Operating Support grant, thanks to a legislative appropriation from the arts and cultural heritage fund. For a full listing of Milkweed Editions supporters, please visit milkweed.org.

Interior design by Mary Austin Speaker
Typeset in Vendetta

Vendetta was designed in 1999 by John Downer for the Emigre type foundry.
The design of Vendetta was influenced by the design of types by Roman
punchcutters who traced their aesthetic lineage to Nicolas Jenson's seminal 1470
text, *De Evangelica Praeparatione*, a work of Christian apologetics written in the
4th century AD by the historian Eusebius.